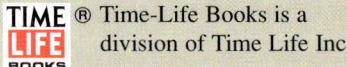 ® Time-Life Books is a
division of Time Life Inc.

TIME LIFE INC.
PRESIDENT and CEO: George Artandi

TIME-LIFE BOOKS
PRESIDENT: John D. Hall
PUBLISHER/MANAGING EDITOR: Neil Kagan

Voices of the Civil War
HISTORICAL DATEBOOK 1997

DIRECTOR, NEW PRODUCT DEVELOPMENT:
Curtis Kopf
MARKETING DIRECTOR: Pamela R. Farrell

Project Editor: Ruth Goldberg
Designer: REDRUTH, Robin Bray, proprietor

Correspondents: Maria Vincenza Aloisi (Paris), Christine Hinze (London), Christina Lieberman (New York).

Vice President, Director of Finance: Christopher Hearing
Vice President, Book Production: Marjann Caldwell
Director of Operations: Eileen Bradley
Director of Photography and Research:
John Conrad Weiser
Director of Editorial Administration: Barbara Levitt
Production Manager: Marlene Zack
Quality Assurance Manager: James King
Library: Louise D. Forstall

Other Publications

HISTORY
The American Story
Voices of the Civil War
The American Indians
Lost Civilizations
Mysteries of the Unknown
Time Frame
The Civil War
Cultural Atlas

COOKING
Weight Watchers® Smart Choice Recipe Collection
Great Taste~Low Fat
Williams-Sonoma Kitchen Library

DO IT YOURSELF
The Time-Life Complete Gardener
Home Repair and Improvement
The Art of Woodworking
Fix It Yourself

TIME-LIFE KIDS
Family Time Bible Stories
Library of First Questions and Answers
A Child's First Library of Learning
I Love Math
Nature Company Discoveries
Understanding Science & Nature

SCIENCE/NATURE
Voyage Through the Universe

For information on and a full description of any of the Time-Life Books series listed above, please call 1-800-621-7026 or write:
Reader Information
Time-Life Customer Service
P.O. Box C-32068
Richmond, Virginia 23261-2068

Front cover: Union general Winfield Scott Hancock poses with Brigadier General Francis C. Barlow, Major General David D. Birney, and Brigadier General John Gibbon.

V★ICES
OF THE
CIVIL WAR

HISTORICAL DATEBOOK
1 9 9 7

BY THE EDITORS OF TIME-LIFE BOOKS ALEXANDRIA, VIRGINIA

Alexander Gardner took this compelling portrait of President Abraham Lincoln in 1863, around the time he wrote the Gettysburg Address. A special edition of the Charleston *Mercury (opposite)* announces the breakup of the Union in response to Lincoln's election.

January

"A house divided against itself cannot stand. I believe this government cannot endure, permanently half slave and half free. I do not expect the union to be dissolved–but I do expect it will become all one thing or all the other."

President Abraham Lincoln, June 16, 1858

WEDNESDAY - NEW YEAR'S DAY
1863 EMANCIPATION PROCLAMATION TAKES EFFECT

1

THURSDAY

2

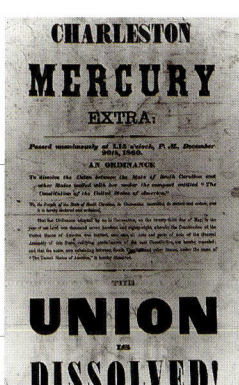

FRIDAY

3

SATURDAY

4

January

SUNDAY

5

MONDAY

6

TUESDAY

7

WEDNESDAY

8

THURSDAY

9

FRIDAY - *1861 FLORIDA SECEDES*

10

SATURDAY - *1861 ALABAMA SECEDES*
1863 ARKANSAS POST (FORT HINDMAN) CAPTURED BY FEDERALS

11

"Captain Taylor administered to me the oath of allegiance to the Confederate States of America and I became a soldier sixteen days before my 18th birthday...How proud I was to be a soldier! To take a man's place in the great conflict! I resolved then that I would never do an act that my good father and mother would be ashamed of."
Isaac N. Rainey, 7th Tennessee Infantry

Members of the Richmond Grays, a company of the 1st Virginia Infantry, pose early in the war.

"*This Southern Confederacy must be supported now by calm determination and cool brains. We have risked all and we must play our best, for the stake is life or death.*"
Mary Chesnut

⬥⬥⬥

Southerner Mary Boykin Chesnut, the Civil War's most famous diarist, poses with her husband, James, in the year of their marriage, 1840. The feather fan *(opposite)* was a gift from President Jefferson Davis on Christmas Day 1863.

JANUARY

SUNDAY

12

MONDAY

13

TUESDAY

14

WEDNESDAY - *1865 Capture of Fort Fisher, Wilmington, North Carolina*

15

THURSDAY

16

FRIDAY

17

SATURDAY

18

January

SUNDAY - *1807 Robert E. Lee born*
19 *1861 Georgia secedes*
1862 Battle of Mill Springs, Kentucky

MONDAY - *Martin Luther King Jr.'s Birthday (observed)*
20

TUESDAY - *1824 Thomas J. "Stonewall" Jackson born*
21

WEDNESDAY
22

THURSDAY
23

FRIDAY
24

SATURDAY
25

A young "powder monkey" poses on the deck of the U.S.S. *Pawnee*, anchored off Charleston, South Carolina. Powder monkeys were young, agile boys who worked aboard warships, running between the ship's magazine and their assigned guns to deliver ammunition and water to gunnery crews under fire.

"The first thing in the morning is drill. Then drill, then drill again. Then drill, drill, a little more drill, then drill, lastly drill."
A Pennsylvania private

Federal officers stand beside a cannon within the walls of Fort Richardson, Virginia, while men of the 1st Connecticut Heavy Artillery drill beyond the fort's walls.

JANUARY-FEBRUARY

SUNDAY
26

MONDAY
27

TUESDAY
28

WEDNESDAY
29

THURSDAY
30

FRIDAY - *1865 ROBERT E. LEE NAMED GENERAL IN CHIEF OF CONFEDERATE ARMIES*
31

SATURDAY - *1861 TEXAS SECEDES*
1

❧ February ❧

SUNDAY

2

MONDAY

3

TUESDAY – *1861 Convention of seceded states meets in Montgomery, Alabama*

4

WEDNESDAY – *1865 Battle of Hatcher's Run, Virginia, begins*

5

THURSDAY – *1862 Surrender of Fort Henry, Tennessee*

6

FRIDAY – *1865 Battle of Hatcher's Run, Virginia, ends*

7

SATURDAY – *1820 William Tecumseh Sherman born*
1862 Battle of Roanoke Island, North Carolina

8

"Once let the black man get upon his person the brass letters, 'U.S.,' let him get an eagle on his buttons and a musket on his shoulder and bullets in his pocket, and there is no power on earth which can deny that he has earned the right to citizenship in the United States."
Frederick Douglass

Abolitionist Frederick Douglass, shown here in 1856, was a tireless advocate for black recruitment into the Union army. His goal was eventually realized in the creation of the all-black 54th Massachusetts Volunteers. Douglass purchased this silver pocket watch *(left)* in Ireland in 1846, on his first lecture tour abroad, and carried it with him all his life.

> *"This regiment has established its reputation as a fighting regiment, not a man flinched, though it was a trying time. Men fell all around me. A shell would explode and clear a space of twenty feet, our men would close up again, but it was no use we had to retreat, which was a very hazardous undertaking. How I got out of that fight alive I cannot tell, but I am here. My dear girl I hope again to see you. I must bid you farewell should I be killed. Remember if I die I die in a good cause. I wish we had a hundred thousand colored troops we would put an end to this war."*
> Lewis Douglass to his fiancée, July 20, 1863

Frederick Douglass's two sons, Sergeant Major Lewis Henry *(left)* and Charles Remond, were among the early enlistees in the 54th Massachusetts Volunteers. Lewis saw heavy fighting in South Carolina in 1863.

FEBRUARY

SUNDAY - *1861 JEFFERSON DAVIS ELECTED PROVISIONAL PRESIDENT OF THE CONFEDERATE STATES*

9

MONDAY

10

TUESDAY

11

WEDNESDAY - ASH WEDNESDAY
1809 ABRAHAM LINCOLN BORN

12

THURSDAY - *1862 FEDERAL ATTACK ON FORT DONELSON, TENNESSEE*

13

FRIDAY - VALENTINE'S DAY
1864 FEDERALS CAPTURE MERIDIAN, MISSISSIPPI

14

SATURDAY

15

February

SUNDAY - *1862 Surrender of Fort Donelson, Tennessee*

16

MONDAY - **PRESIDENTS' DAY**
1865 Federals capture and burn Columbia, South Carolina

17

TUESDAY - *1861 Jefferson Davis inaugurated provisional president of the Confederacy*

18

WEDNESDAY

19

THURSDAY - *1864 Battle of Olustee (Ocean Pond), Florida*

20

FRIDAY - *1862 Engagement at Valverde, New Mexico Territory*

21

SATURDAY - *1864 Engagement at Okolona, Mississippi*

22

"The audience was large and brilliant. Upon my weary heart was showered smiles, plaudits and flowers, but beyond them, I saw trouble and thorns innumerable."
Jefferson Davis, writing to his wife after his inauguration

Kentucky-born Jefferson Davis was inaugurated provisional president of the Confederate States of America on February 18, 1861. Davis had served as secretary of war under Franklin Pierce and as a congressman and senator from Mississippi.

"The moment the troops were put into position to go into camp all the men connected with this branch of service would proceed to put up their wires. A mule loaded with a coil of wire would be led to the rear of the nearest flank of the brigade he belonged to, and would be led in a line parallel thereto, while one man would hold an end of the wire and uncoil it as the mule was led off...This would be done in the rear of every brigade at the same time. The ends of all the wires would be joined, making a continuous wire in the rear of the whole army. The men, attached to brigades or divisions, would all commence at once raising the wires with their telegraph poles...While this was being done the telegraph wagons would take their positions near where the headquarters they belonged to were to be established, and would connect with the wire. Thus, in a few minutes longer time than it took a mule to walk the length of its coil, telegraphic communication would be effected between all the headquarters of the army."

Ulysses S. Grant describing the set-up of telegraph wires

The Federal Telegraph Construction Corps *(top)* puts up wire in April 1864. Telegraph operators *(bottom)* perform their jobs at a field station on the James River at Wilcox's Landing, Virginia.

February-March

SUNDAY
23

MONDAY
24

TUESDAY – *1862 Federal troops occupy Nashville, Tennessee*
25

WEDNESDAY
26

THURSDAY
27

FRIDAY
28

SATURDAY
1

MARCH

SUNDAY

2

MONDAY

3

TUESDAY - *1861 ABRAHAM LINCOLN INAUGURATED PRESIDENT OF THE UNITED STATES*
1865 LINCOLN'S SECOND INAUGURATION

4

WEDNESDAY

5

THURSDAY

6

FRIDAY

7

SATURDAY - *1862 C.S.S. VIRGINIA DESTROYS FEDERAL WARSHIPS CONGRESS AND CUMBERLAND*

8

"You cannot make soldiers of slaves or slaves of soldiers...And if slaves seem good soldiers, then our whole theory of slavery is wrong." Major General Howell Cobb of Georgia, responding to the idea of enlisting slaves in the Confederate army

The provost guard of the 107th Colored Infantry pose at Fort Corcoran, near Washington, D.C.

"The most profound silence reigned. If there had been a coward's heart there its throb would have been audible, so intense was the stillness. We were enclosed in what we supposed to be an impenetrable armor. We knew that a powerful foe was about to meet us. Ours was an untried experiment and our enemy's first fire might make it a coffin for us all."

Paymaster William Keeler, U.S.S. *Monitor*

"No words can express the surprise with which we beheld this strange craft, whose appearance was tersely and graphically described by the exclamation of one of my oarsmen, 'A tin can on a shingle!'"

A Confederate observer of the battle between the *Virginia* and the *Monitor*

This photograph of officers and crew on the U.S.S. *Monitor* was taken at Hampton Roads, Virginia, in July 1862. The engagement of the *Monitor* and the *Virginia* on March 9, 1862, the first battle between two ironclad ships, marked a breakthrough in naval warfare.

~ MARCH ~

SUNDAY - *1862 Battle between C.S.S. Virginia and U.S.S. Monitor*
1864 General Ulysses S. Grant commissioned lieutenant general and appointed commander of Federal armies

9

MONDAY

10

TUESDAY - *1865 Federal troops capture Fayetteville, North Carolina*

11

WEDNESDAY - *1864 Beginning of the Red River campaign, Louisiana*

12

THURSDAY

13

FRIDAY - *1862 Federals capture New Madrid, Missouri, and New Bern, North Carolina*
1863 Federal gunboats pass Port Hudson, Louisiana

14

SATURDAY

15

March

Sunday
16

Monday - Saint Patrick's Day
1863 Battle of Kelly's Ford, Virginia
17

Tuesday
18

Wednesday
19

Thursday
20

Friday
21

Saturday
22

"Every man has a sprig of green in his cap, and a half-laughing half-murderous look in his eye."
Federal officer describing the Irish Brigade

Five members of Brigadier General Thomas F. Meagher's Irish Brigade are shown in camp at Harrison's Landing in July 1862. On December 13, 1862, at the Battle of Fredericksburg, many of Meagher's men were shot down by Irishmen of Colonel Robert McMillan's 24th Georgia Infantry. One of Meagher's regiments, the 28th Massachusetts, carried the flag (*opposite*) at Fredericksburg. The Gaelic inscription means "Clear the way."

Harper's Weekly artist Alfred R. Waud poses on July 6, 1863, for photographer Timothy O'Sullivan at Gettysburg. The Waud sketch at right depicts two black teamsters of the Federal army smoking bacon at Brandy Station, Virginia.

MARCH

SUNDAY - *1862 BATTLE OF KERNSTOWN, VIRGINIA*

23

MONDAY

24

TUESDAY

25

WEDNESDAY - *1862 ENGAGEMENT AT APACHE CANYON, NEW MEXICO TERRITORY*

26

THURSDAY

27

FRIDAY - *GOOD FRIDAY*
1862 BATTLE OF GLORIETTA PASS, NEW MEXICO TERRITORY

28

SATURDAY

29

March-April

Sunday - Easter
30

Monday
31

Tuesday
1

Wednesday - *1865 Confederate government evacuates Richmond*
2

Thursday - *1863 Bread riots in Richmond*
1865 Federal troops enter Richmond and Petersburg, Virginia
3

Friday - *1865 President Abraham Lincoln visits Richmond*
4

Saturday - *1862 Siege of Yorktown, Virginia, begins*
5

A Southern family, caught in the path of the war, prepares to flee with its belongings.

"...a heartrending scene. Women searching for their babies along the road, where they had been lost; others sitting in the dust and crying and wringing their hands. All the talk was of burning homes, houses knocked to pieces by balls, famine, murder, desolation."

Young woman fleeing Baton Rouge

"O it was too shocking, too horrible! God grant that I may never partake in such scenes again. When released from this I shall ever be an advocate of peace."
Confederate soldier describing the Battle of Shiloh

Gun crews of Battery B of the 2d Illinois Light Artillery stand beside five 24-pounder siege guns that helped them fight off Confederate troops during the Battle of Shiloh a few days earlier. The bugle opposite was shot from the hand of Indiana private Frederick Barnhart as he sounded the call to battle.

April

SUNDAY - *DAYLIGHT-SAVING TIME BEGINS*
1862 BATTLE OF SHILOH begins

6

MONDAY - *1862 BATTLE OF SHILOH ends*
1863 UNSUCCESSFUL FEDERAL naval attack on CHARLESTON, SOUTH CAROLINA

7

TUESDAY - *1864 BATTLE OF SABINE CROSSROADS, LOUISIANA*

8

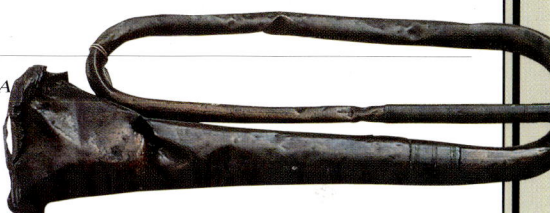

WEDNESDAY - *1865 ARMY OF NORTHERN VIRGINIA surrenders at APPOMATTOX COURT HOUSE, VIRGINIA*

9

THURSDAY

10

FRIDAY - *1862 CAPTURE OF FORT PULASKI, GEORGIA*
1865 SURRENDER OF MOBILE, ALABAMA

11

SATURDAY

12

April

SUNDAY - *1861 Fort Sumter, South Carolina, surrenders to Confederates*

13

MONDAY - *1865 President Abraham Lincoln assassinated at Ford's Theatre*
Federal flag raised at Fort Sumter

14

TUESDAY - *1865 Death of Lincoln. Andrew Johnson takes oath as president*

15

WEDNESDAY - *1863 Admiral David D. Porter's Federal fleet passes Vicksburg*

16

THURSDAY - *1861 Virginia Convention votes for secession*

17

FRIDAY - *1862 Federal fleet bombards Forts Jackson and St. Philip near New Orleans*

18

SATURDAY - *1861 Riots in Baltimore*

19

> *"Civil war is actually upon us, and strange to say, it brings a feeling of relief: the suspense is over."* Senator John Sherman of Ohio, responding to the events at Fort Sumter

Following the successful siege of Fort Sumter in April 1861, Confederate dignitaries inspect a cannon on the fort's parade ground. The Union flag *(opposite)* flew over the fort during the 33-hour bombardment. When a Rebel shell destroyed the flag's pole, Federal troops raised the flag again by nailing it to a spar.

"It is well that war is so terrible. We should grow too fond of it."
General Robert E. Lee

General Robert E. Lee sat for this somber portrait in April 1865, shortly after his surrender at Appomattox. He sits on the porch of his Richmond home with his son, Major General George Washington Custis Lee *(left),* and aide Colonel Walter Taylor.

April

SUNDAY - *1861 Robert E. Lee is confirmed as commander of Virginia forces*

20

MONDAY - *Passover*

21

TUESDAY

22

WEDNESDAY

23

THURSDAY

24

FRIDAY - *1862 Surrender of New Orleans, Louisiana*

25

SATURDAY

26

April-May

SUNDAY - *1822 ULYSSES S. GRANT BORN*

27

MONDAY

28

TUESDAY - *1861 MARYLAND HOUSE OF DELEGATES OPPOSES SECESSION*

29

WEDNESDAY

30

THURSDAY - *1863 BATTLE OF CHANCELLORSVILLE, VIRGINIA, BEGINS*

1

FRIDAY - *1863 LIEUTENANT GENERAL THOMAS J. "STONEWALL" JACKSON WOUNDED*

2

SATURDAY - *1863 SECOND BATTLE OF FREDERICKSBURG AND BATTLE OF SALEM CHURCH, VIRGINIA*

3

*"At Chancellorsville we gained another victory, our
people were wild with delight. I, on the contrary, was more depressed
than after Fredericksburg; our losses were severe, and again we had
gained not an inch of ground, and the enemy could not be pursued."*
General Robert E. Lee

Pickets of Brigadier General William Barksdale's Mississippi brigade stand on the remains of a wrecked railroad bridge at Fredericksburg, just days before the Battle of Chancellorsville. This image was taken from across the Rappahannock by Union photographer Andrew J. Russell.

"Presently a smile...spread itself over his pale face, and he said quietly, and with an expression as if of relief, 'Let us cross over the river and rest under the shade of the trees.'"
Dr. Hunter McGuire describing General Jackson's death

Lieutenant General Stonewall Jackson, whom Robert E. Lee considered his right-hand man, was accidentally shot by his own men on May 2, 1863, at Chancellorsville. He died on May 10.

MAY

SUNDAY

4

MONDAY - *1864 Battle of the Wilderness (Virginia) begins*

5

TUESDAY - *1861 Arkansas and Tennessee pass secession ordinances*
1864 Battle of the Wilderness ends

6

WEDNESDAY - *1864 Federals under Major General William T. Sherman begin Atlanta campaign*

7

THURSDAY - *1862 Battle of McDowell, Virginia*

8

FRIDAY - *1862 Evacuation of Norfolk by Confederates*

9

SATURDAY - *1861 Riots in St. Louis, Missouri*
1863 Death of Lieutenant General Thomas J. "Stonewall" Jackson

10

MAY

SUNDAY - MOTHER'S DAY
11
1864 BATTLE OF YELLOW TAVERN, VIRGINIA. MAJOR GENERAL JAMES EWELL BROWN "JEB" STUART MORTALLY WOUNDED

MONDAY - *1863 ENGAGEMENT AT RAYMOND, MISSISSIPPI*
12

TUESDAY - *1861 FEDERAL TROOPS OCCUPY BALTIMORE, MARYLAND*
13

WEDNESDAY - *1863 ENGAGEMENT AT JACKSON, MISSISSIPPI*
14

THURSDAY
15

FRIDAY - *1863 BATTLE OF CHAMPION'S HILL, MISSISSIPPI*
16

SATURDAY - *1863 ENGAGEMENT AT BIG BLACK RIVER, MISSISSIPPI*
17

"He never brought me a false piece of information."
Robert E. Lee about Major General Jeb Stuart

Robert E. Lee called his cavalry commander, Major General Jeb Stuart, "the eyes of the Army" for his scouting prowess. Stuart, a brilliant leader, was revered by soldiers and civilians alike.

"It was the heart-break of the Southern Confederacy."

Major Henry Kyd Douglas, describing the reaction to General Jackson's death

A group of mourners lament at Stonewall Jackson's grave. Jackson was buried at the Virginia Military Institute, where he had taught before the war.

May

Sunday - 1863 Siege of Vicksburg, Mississippi, begins

18

Monday - 1863 First assault on Vicksburg

19

Tuesday - 1861 North Carolina secedes
1862 Federal Homestead Law signed

20

Wednesday - 1863 Siege of Port Hudson, Louisiana, begins

21

Thursday - 1863 Second assault on Vicksburg

22

Friday - 1862 Engagement at Front Royal, Virginia

23

Saturday - 1861 Federal troops occupy Alexandria, Virginia

24

MAY

SUNDAY - *1862 BATTLE OF WINCHESTER, VIRGINIA*

25

MONDAY - *MEMORIAL DAY*

26

TUESDAY - *1863 FIRST ASSAULT ON PORT HUDSON, LOUISIANA*

27

WEDNESDAY

28

THURSDAY

29

FRIDAY - *1862 CONFEDERATES EVACUATE CORINTH, MISSISSIPPI*

30

SATURDAY - *1862 BATTLE OF FAIR OAKS (SEVEN PINES), VIRGINIA*

31

A crew inflates the Union observation balloon *Intrepid* on June 1, 1862, so that Professor Thaddeus C. Lowe can observe the Battle of Fair Oaks. Inset, the men let out the balloon's mooring ropes as Lowe ascends. Lowe employed three such balloons, each with a crew of 30 to 50, during the Peninsula campaign.

"With the aid of good glasses we were enabled to view the whole affair between these powerful contending armies...Occasionally a masked Rebel battery would open upon our brave fellows. In such cases the occupants of the balloon would inform our artillerists of its position, and the next shot or two would, in every case, silence the masked and annoying customer."
Union reporter describing an observation flight over the Battle of Fair Oaks, Virginia

Lieutenant General Ulysses S. Grant holds an open-air war council outside Massaponax Church, Virginia, on May 21, 1864, days before the Battle of Cold Harbor. Timothy O'Sullivan shot the unusual series of photographs from the second story, front window of the church. Grant can be seen leaning over the shoulder of General George G. Meade on one of the pews removed from the church.

J∼ UNE ∼

SUNDAY - *1864 Battle of Cold Harbor, Virginia, begins*

1

MONDAY

2

TUESDAY - *1808 Jefferson Davis born*
1861 Fighting at Philippi, Virginia
1864 Battle of Cold Harbor ends

3

WEDNESDAY

4

THURSDAY

5

FRIDAY - *1862 Battle of Memphis, Tennessee*

6

SATURDAY

7

JUNE

SUNDAY - *1864 PRESIDENT ABRAHAM LINCOLN NOMINATED FOR A SECOND TERM*

8

MONDAY - *1862 BATTLE OF PORT REPUBLIC, VIRGINIA*
1863 BATTLE OF BRANDY STATION, VIRGINIA

9

TUESDAY - *1861 ENGAGEMENT AT BIG BETHEL, VIRGINIA*

10

WEDNESDAY

11

THURSDAY

12

FRIDAY

13

SATURDAY - *FLAG DAY*
1863 BATTLE OF SECOND WINCHESTER, VIRGINIA, AND
SECOND ASSAULT ON PORT HUDSON, LOUISIANA

14

"I regard all these newspaper harpies as spies and think they should be punished as such."

Major General William Tecumseh Sherman

This image shows the headquarters of the New York *Herald* in the field at Bealton, Virginia, in August 1863. Ironically, reports filed by hundreds of correspondents who covered the war for Northern newspapers often provided useful information to Confederate generals. Although Union generals complained of press leaks, none was more outspoken in his hatred of reporters than General William Sherman.

"*Vicksburg must not be lost, at least without a struggle. The interest and honor of the Confederacy forbid it.*"
Confederate Secretary of War James A. Seddon,
June 16, 1863

A house used as quarters for Union troops during the siege of Vicksburg looks over a hillside riddled with shelters dug by the 45th Illinois to shield them from Confederate artillery. The house was abandoned by a family who, like many others, fled to a cave during the Union siege of Vicksburg in June 1863.

JUNE

SUNDAY - FATHER'S DAY

15

MONDAY - *1862 ENGAGEMENT AT SECESSIONVILLE (JAMES ISLAND), SOUTH CAROLINA*
1864 FEDERALS BEGIN SIEGE OF PETERSBURG, VIRGINIA

16

TUESDAY - *1861 ENGAGEMENT AT BOONVILLE, MISSOURI*

17

WEDNESDAY

18

THURSDAY - *1862 LINCOLN SIGNS LAW PROHIBITING SLAVERY IN THE TERRITORIES*

19

FRIDAY

20

SATURDAY

21

JUNE

SUNDAY
22

MONDAY - *1863 Tullahoma campaign begins in Tennessee*
23

TUESDAY
24

WEDNESDAY - *1862 Beginning of the Seven Days' Battles outside Richmond, Virginia*
25

THURSDAY - *1862 Battle of Mechanicsville (Beaver Dam Creek), Virginia*
26

FRIDAY - *1862 Battle of Gaines' Mill (First Cold Harbor), Virginia*
27

SATURDAY - *1862 Admiral David G. Farragut's Federal fleet passes Vicksburg, Mississippi*
28

> *"There are times when a corps commander's life does not count."*
> Major General Winfield Scott Hancock at Gettysburg

Called Hancock the Superb by his peers, Union general Winfield Scott Hancock *(seated)* poses with three of his division commanders: *(left to right)* Brigadier General Francis C. Barlow, Major General David D. Birney, and Brigadier General John Gibbon. Hancock played a crucial role at Gettysburg and on July 3, 1863, was severely wounded during the repulse of Pickett's Charge.

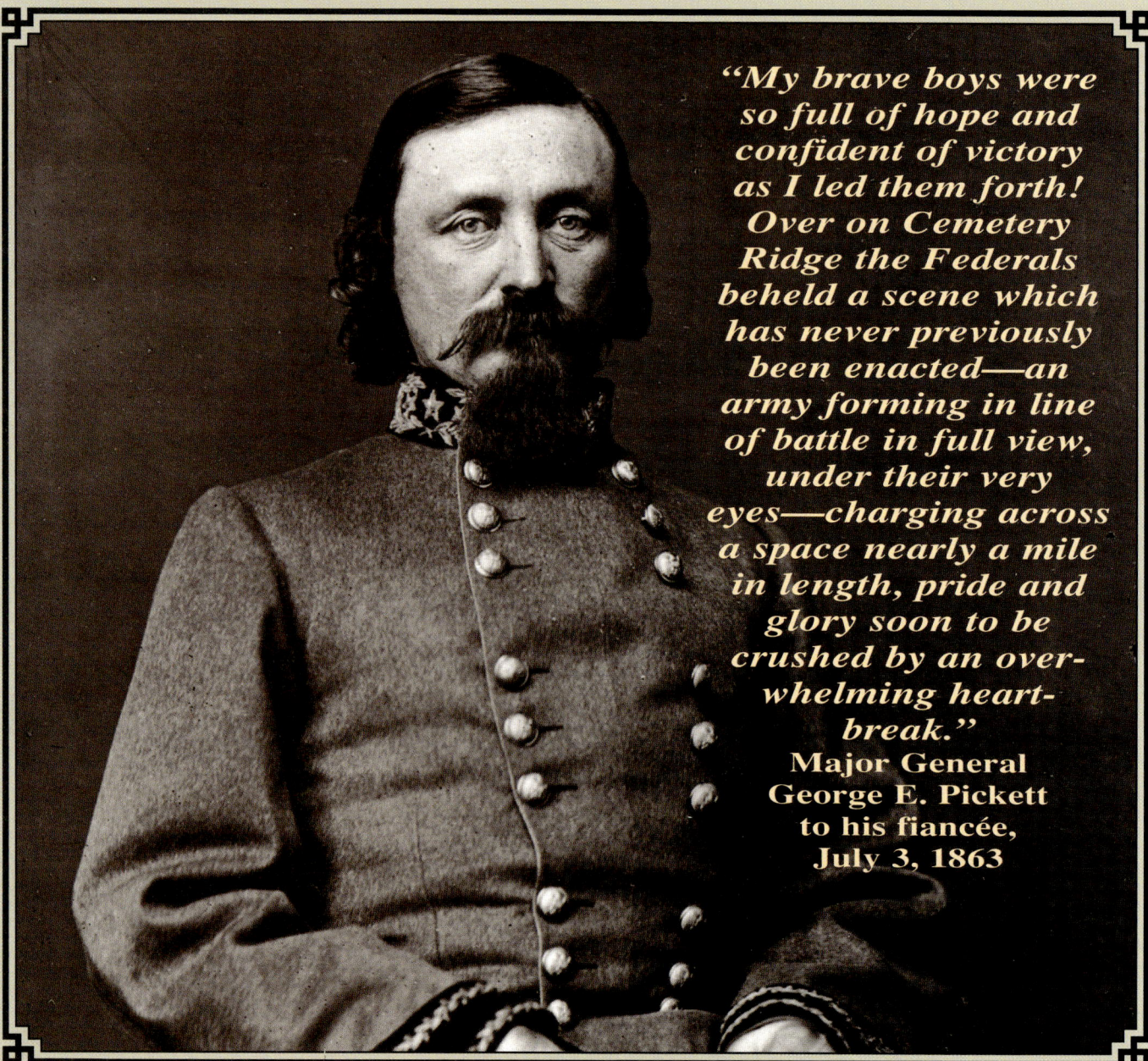

"My brave boys were so full of hope and confident of victory as I led them forth! Over on Cemetery Ridge the Federals beheld a scene which has never previously been enacted—an army forming in line of battle in full view, under their very eyes—charging across a space nearly a mile in length, pride and glory soon to be crushed by an over-whelming heart-break."
Major General George E. Pickett to his fiancée, July 3, 1863

The division commanded by Major General George E. Pickett was decimated in the disastrous Confederate assault at Gettysburg on July 3, 1863, that marked the turning point of the war. Afterward, Lee's army retreated from the North, never to return. Pickett never forgave Lee for ordering the doomed maneuver.

June-July

Sunday

29

Monday - *1862 Battle of Frayser's Farm (White Oak Swamp), Virginia*

30

Tuesday - *1862 Battle at Malvern Hill, Virginia*
1863 Battle of Gettysburg, Pennsylvania, begins

1

Wednesday

2

Thursday - *1863 Battle of Gettysburg, Pennsylvania, ends*

3

Friday - *Independence Day*
1861 Lincoln calls special session of Congress to pass war measures
1863 Surrender of Vicksburg, Mississippi

4

Saturday - *1861 Engagement at Carthage, Missouri*

5

 JULY

SUNDAY

6

MONDAY

7

TUESDAY - *1863 Surrender of Port Hudson, Louisiana*

8

WEDNESDAY

9

THURSDAY

10

FRIDAY - *1861 Engagement at Rich Mountain, Virginia*
1862 Major General Henry W. Halleck appointed general in chief of U.S. armies

11

SATURDAY

12

"Occasionally a shell would come flying over Round Top and explode high in the air over head... The Cannonading, which all the time appeared to be getting more and more severe, lasted until the close of day. It seemed as though the heavens were sending forth peal upon peal of terrible thunder, directly over our heads; while at the same time, the very earth beneath our feet trembled."

Tillie Pierce, describing the second day of the Battle of Gettysburg

Gettysburg resident Tillie Pierce was 15 years old when this photograph was taken in 1863. During the Battle of Gettysburg, her parents sent her to the Weikert farm, on the outskirts of town, for safety. But she found herself even closer to the action. She later wrote a book about the experience.

Three Confederate soldiers captured at Gettysburg lean against a rail-and-timber breastwork
on Seminary Ridge, while awaiting transport to a prison camp.

*"While I was sitting on a little stump, the fellows were sitting around and standing around every-
where, old General Kilpatrick in command of the Yankee cavalry, rode up close to the fence, and
hollered out, 'Attention Prisoners. If you behave yourselves and don't try to get away, I will treat
you as prisoners of war, but if you attempt to escape, I'll order my cavalry to charge right and
left, and hew you down.' Some fool prisoner hollered out, 'Three cheers for Jeff Davis.' and you
never heard such a yell on earth. The old General rode off."*
Colonel John A. Fite, 7th Tennessee Infantry, captured July 3, 1863, at Gettysburg

JULY

SUNDAY - 1863 DRAFT RIOTS IN NEW YORK CITY

13

MONDAY - 1864 BATTLE OF TUPELO, MISSISSIPPI

14

TUESDAY - 1862 C.S.S. ARKANSAS ATTACKS FEDERAL FLEET NORTH OF VICKSBURG, MISSISSIPPI

15

WEDNESDAY

16

THURSDAY - 1862 CONFISCATION ACT SIGNED BY LINCOLN

17

FRIDAY - 1861 ENGAGEMENT AT BLACKBURN'S FORD, VIRGINIA

18

SATURDAY

19

JULY

SUNDAY
20

MONDAY - *1861 First Battle of Manassas (Bull Run)*
21

TUESDAY - *1862 Lincoln presents Emancipation Proclamation to cabinet*
1864 Battle of Atlanta, Georgia
22

WEDNESDAY
23

THURSDAY
24

FRIDAY
25

SATURDAY - *1861 Federals surrender Fort Fillmore in New Mexico Territory*
26

"If it is necessary that I should fall on the battlefield for my country, I am ready. I have no misgivings about, or lack of confidence in, the cause in which I am engaged, and my courage does not halt or falter."

Major Sullivan Ballou, July 14, 1861, a week before his death at the First Battle of Manassas

A lone figure rests against what remains of the frame of the Henry house, which was destroyed by Union artillery during the First Battle of Manassas on July 21, 1861.

Private Edwin F. Jemison
of Company C, 2d Louisi-
ana Infantry, was killed at
Malvern Hill, Virginia, on
July 1, 1862.

July-August

SUNDAY
27

MONDAY
28

TUESDAY
29

WEDNESDAY
30

THURSDAY - *1861 Ulysses S. Grant appointed brigadier general*
31

FRIDAY
1

SATURDAY
2

~ AUGUST ~

SUNDAY

3

MONDAY

4

TUESDAY – *1862 ENGAGEMENT AT BATON ROUGE, LOUISIANA*
1864 BATTLE OF MOBILE BAY, ALABAMA

5

WEDNESDAY – *1862 C.S.S. ARKANSAS LOST IN ACTION*

6

THURSDAY – *1864 SURRENDER OF FORT GAINES IN MOBILE BAY, ALABAMA*

7

FRIDAY

8

SATURDAY – *1862 BATTLE OF CEDAR MOUNTAIN, VIRGINIA*

9

> *"...if heaven ever sent out a homely angel, she must be one, her assistance was so timely."*
> Surgeon's description of Clara Barton

A nurse tends wounded Confederates captured at Gettysburg. Clara Barton *(opposite)* first experienced the horrors of war while nursing in August 1862 at the Battle of Cedar Mountain. Known as the Angel of the Battlefield, she went on to organize the American Red Cross in 1881.

A Federal sentry checks a soldier's pass before allowing him to board the Georgetown ferry, which traveled from Analostan Island across the Potomac River to Washington, D.C. During the war, security was tight at all points of entry to the Federal capital, to guard against Confederate spies as well as Union deserters.

AUGUST

SUNDAY - *1861 Battle of Wilson's Creek, Missouri*

10

MONDAY

11

TUESDAY

12

WEDNESDAY

13

THURSDAY

14

FRIDAY

15

SATURDAY

16

AUGUST

SUNDAY – *1862 Sioux uprising begins in Minnesota*

17

MONDAY

18

TUESDAY

19

WEDNESDAY

20

THURSDAY

21

FRIDAY

22

SATURDAY

23

"I was unwilling to abandon the ground as long as I saw a shadow of probability of victory; the troops would, I believed, return better satisfied even after defeat if, in grasping at the last straw, they felt that a brave and vigorous effort had been made to save the country from disaster." Major General John Bell Hood after his defeat at the Battle of Nashville

Major General John Bell Hood, who stood six feet two inches tall, lost the use of an arm at Gettysburg and a leg at Chickamauga and thereafter had to be strapped into his saddle. He assumed command of the Army of Tennessee from General Joseph E. Johnston on July 17, 1864.

"Kiss the little ones for me, and assure yourself I will do all I can to save myself consistent with honor."
Lieutenant Colonel
Joseph A. McLean to his wife,
August 22, 1862

Lieutenant Colonel Joseph A. McLean of the 88th Pennsylvania Infantry was killed at Chinn Ridge during the Battle of Second Manassas on August 30, 1862. His body was never recovered.

AUGUST

SUNDAY - *1862 C.S.S. Alabama commissioned off the Azores*

24

MONDAY

25

TUESDAY - *1862 Battle of Second Manassas (Second Bull Run), Virginia, begins*

26

WEDNESDAY

27

THURSDAY - *1861 Capture of Fort Hatteras, North Carolina, by Federals*
1862 Battle of Brawner's Farm (Groveton), Virginia

28

FRIDAY

29

SATURDAY - *1861 Federal general John C. Frémont issues local emancipation proclamation in Missouri*
1862 Battle of Second Manassas (Second Bull Run), Virginia, ends

30

AUGUST-SEPTEMBER

SUNDAY
31

MONDAY - LABOR DAY
1862 BATTLE OF CHANTILLY (OX HILL), VIRGINIA
1

TUESDAY - *1864 FEDERAL TROOPS ENTER ATLANTA*
2

WEDNESDAY
3

THURSDAY
4

FRIDAY
5

SATURDAY - *1861 FEDERAL GUNBOATS CAPTURE PADUCAH, KENTUCKY*
6

*"One of my super-
stitions had always
been when I started
to go anywhere or
to do anything, not
to turn back or to
stop until the thing
was accomplished."*
Lieutenant General
Ulysses S. Grant

This portrait of Ulysses S. Grant was taken shortly after he was commissioned lieutenant general of the U.S. Army.

"Atlanta is gone. That agony is over. There is no hope but we will try to have no fear."
Mary Chesnut

The wreckage of a Confederate ordnance train is strewn in front of the remains of a mill used for rolling sheet metal. Both were destroyed by the same blast, set off on September 1, 1864, by Major General John Bell Hood's Confederate cavalrymen as they prepared to abandon Atlanta. They destroyed 81 carloads of ammunition and several locomotives to keep them from falling into Union hands.

SEPTEMBER

SUNDAY

7

MONDAY

8

TUESDAY

9

WEDNESDAY - 1863 FEDERALS CAPTURE LITTLE ROCK, ARKANSAS

10

THURSDAY - 1861 CHEAT MOUNTAIN CAMPAIGN, IN WESTERN VIRGINIA, BEGINS

11

FRIDAY - 1861 SIEGE OF LEXINGTON, MISSOURI, BEGINS

12

SATURDAY

13

September

SUNDAY

14

MONDAY – *1861 Cheat Mountain campaign, in western Virginia, ends*
1862 Confederates under Lieutenant General Thomas J. "Stonewall"
Jackson capture Harpers Ferry, Virginia

15

TUESDAY

16

WEDNESDAY – *1862 Battle of Antietam (Sharpsburg), Maryland*

17

THURSDAY

18

FRIDAY – *1862 Battle of Iuka, Mississippi*
1863 Battle of Chickamauga, Georgia, begins

19

SATURDAY – *1861 Surrender of Lexington, Missouri*
1863 Battle of Chickamauga ends

20

> *"I have heard of the 'dead lying in heaps,'*
> *but never saw it till this battle.*
> *Whole ranks fell together."*
> Captain Emory Upton,
> 2d U.S. Artillery, at Antietam

The simple headboard in the foreground of this Alexander Gardner photograph marks the grave of Private John Marshall of Company L, 28th Pennsylvania Volunteers, on the battlefield at Antietam.

"He was an expert drummer, and being a bright, cheery child, soon made his way into the affection of officers and soldiers."
Johnny Clem's sister

Drummer Johnny Clem ran away to join the Union army before he was 10 years old. Celebrated as the Drummer Boy of Chickamauga for shooting and wounding a Confederate officer during that battle, he went on to serve in the postwar army until 1915, when he retired as a major general. He was the last active serviceman to have fought in the Civil War.

S EPTEMBER

SUNDAY
21

MONDAY - *1862 Emancipation Proclamation issued*
22

TUESDAY - *1864 Battle of Fisher's Hill, Virginia*
23

WEDNESDAY
24

THURSDAY
25

FRIDAY
26

SATURDAY
27

SUNDAY
28

MONDAY
29

TUESDAY
30

WEDNESDAY
1

THURSDAY - ROSH HASHANAH
2

FRIDAY - *1862 Battle of Corinth, Mississippi, begins*
3

SATURDAY - *1862 Battle of Corinth ends*
4

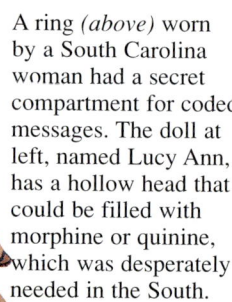

A ring *(above)* worn by a South Carolina woman had a secret compartment for coded messages. The doll at left, named Lucy Ann, has a hollow head that could be filled with morphine or quinine, which was desperately needed in the South.

"But for you, there would have been no Bull Run." Jefferson Davis to Rose Greenhow upon her release from prison

Widow Rose O'Neal Greenhow and her daughter, "Little Rose," are shown in 1862 at the Old Capitol building in Washington, D.C. where Greenhow was confined for her alleged activities as a Confederate spy. Greenhow was released and sent South on June 2 of that year. On September 30, 1864, Rose Greenhow was returning from France when she was drowned in the wreck of the blockade runner *Condor* off the coast of North Carolina.

Two future generals, Captain James W. Forsyth *(seated, far left)* and First Lieutenant George Armstrong Custer *(reclining, right),* relax with other Federal officers at Cumberland Landing, Virginia, in July 1862.

OCTOBER

SUNDAY - *1864 Engagement at Allatoona, Georgia*

5

MONDAY

6

TUESDAY

7

WEDNESDAY - *1862 Battle of Perryville, Kentucky*

8

THURSDAY

9

FRIDAY

10

SATURDAY - *Yom Kippur*

11

OCTOBER

SUNDAY
12

MONDAY - COLUMBUS DAY
13

TUESDAY
14

WEDNESDAY
15

THURSDAY
16

FRIDAY
17

SATURDAY
18

In the fall of 1863, Federal cavalry soldiers camp on a hillside in front of Castle Murray, near Auburn, Virginia. The castle was the home of a local doctor, after whom it was named.

Black workers from the U.S. Military Railroad Construction Corps gather for a portrait at the Alexandria wharf in Virginia. Although they were not able to enlist in the Union army until the fall of 1862, blacks labored in large numbers in the Union war effort.

October

SUNDAY
19

MONDAY
20

TUESDAY - *1861 Battle of Ball's Bluff, Virginia*
21

WEDNESDAY
22

THURSDAY - *1864 Battle of Westport, Missouri*
23

FRIDAY - *1861 Transcontinental telegraph completed*
24

SATURDAY
25

October-November

Sunday - Daylight-saving time ends
26

Monday
27

Tuesday
28

Wednesday
29

Thursday
30

Friday - Halloween
31

Saturday - 1861 George B. McClellan appointed Federal general in chief
1

"The true course in conducting military operations is to make no movement until the preparations are as complete as circumstances will permit and never to fight a battle without some definite object worth the probable loss; such a course will ever insure the greatest economy of life, time and treasure, as well as the most decisive results."
Major General
George B. McClellan

Despite his gift for organizing and training the Federal armies, Major General George B. McClellan was finally relieved of command by President Lincoln because of his inability to take decisive action after the Battle of Antietam in 1862.

"*Our men took another night of suffering from the enclemence of the wether which was still rainey and coald but our boys stood the hardships and exposier remarkable well.*"

Private Ira Gillaspie, 11th Michigan Infantry, December 1862

Federal pickets warm themselves around a campfire.

∾ November ∾

SUNDAY

2

MONDAY

3

TUESDAY

4

WEDNESDAY

5

THURSDAY - *1860 Lincoln elected president*

6

FRIDAY - *1861 Battle of Port Royal Sound, South Carolina*

7

SATURDAY - *1864 Lincoln reelected president*

8

November

SUNDAY
9

MONDAY
10

TUESDAY - VETERANS DAY
11

WEDNESDAY
12

THURSDAY
13

FRIDAY
14

SATURDAY
15

"You cannot qualify war in harsher terms than I will. War is cruelty and you cannot refine it, and those who brought war into our country deserve all the curses and maledictions a people can pour out."
**Major General
William Tecumseh Sherman**

Major General Sherman sits on his horse in September 1864, after the capture of Atlanta. Sherman targeted Atlanta for destruction because its factories supplied the Confederate armies with weapons, ammunition, clothing, and other supplies, and because four main rail lines converged there.

New York chaplain Father Thomas H. Mooney says Sunday morning mass for the 69th New York State Militia
in camp near Washington, D.C., in May 1861.

"The whole camp is one religious gathering, and all men seemed greatly interested. There was a grand and glorious awakening.
Many in the spring of 1863 found the blessed savior precious to their souls and rejoiced in his love, I among the number.
Lieutenant David E. Johnston, 7th Virginia Infantry, describing the religious affinities of his comrades

November

SUNDAY - *1864 MAJOR GENERAL WILLIAM T. SHERMAN STARTS MARCH TO THE SEA*

16

MONDAY

17

TUESDAY

18

WEDNESDAY - *1863 PRESIDENT ABRAHAM LINCOLN DELIVERS GETTYSBURG ADDRESS*

19

THURSDAY

20

FRIDAY

21

SATURDAY

22

November

SUNDAY

23

MONDAY - *1863 Battle of Lookout Mountain (Chattanooga, Tennessee)*

24

TUESDAY - *1863 Battle of Missionary Ridge (Chattanooga, Tennessee)*

25

WEDNESDAY

26

THURSDAY - *Thanksgiving*

27

FRIDAY

28

SATURDAY

29

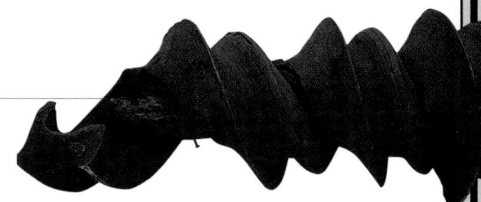

Union soldiers comply with Major General William Tecumseh Sherman's orders to destroy the rail lines that converged at Atlanta. Rails were heated, then twisted out of shape to form what some called "Sherman's hairpins" or "Sherman's bowties." The section of rail opposite still grips the pole it was wrapped around.

"We have been tearing up some more Rail Road and utterly destroying evry thing in the City that can be of any use to the Armies of the South...I don't think any people will want to try and live there now."
Private Theodore F. Upson, 100th Indiana Infantry,
October 9, 1864

Cannonballs line the banks of the James River in front of the ruins of Richmond, photographed by Andrew J. Russell in April 1865.
Fires burned the industrial district but spared the state capitol building.

"Richmond has fallen—and I have no heart to write about it...They are too many for us. Everything lost in Richmond, even our archives. Blue-black is our horizon."
Mary Chesnut

November-December

SUNDAY - *1864 BATTLE OF FRANKLIN, TENNESSEE*

30

MONDAY - *1861 U. S. CONGRESS CREATES THE JOINT COMMITTEE ON THE CONDUCT OF THE WAR*

1

TUESDAY

2

WEDNESDAY

3

THURSDAY

4

FRIDAY

5

SATURDAY

6

December

SUNDAY - *1862 Battle of Prairie Grove, Arkansas*

7

MONDAY - *1863 Lincoln issues Proclamation of Amnesty and Reconstruction*

8

TUESDAY

9

WEDNESDAY

10

THURSDAY

11

FRIDAY

12

SATURDAY - *1862 Battle of Fredericksburg, Virginia*
1864 Federals capture Fort McAllister
(near Savannah, Georgia)

13

> *"The war began in my front yard and ended in my parlor."*
> Wilmer McLean

Ulysses S. Grant accepted Robert E. Lee's surrender at the Appomattox, Virginia, home *(above)* of Wilmer McLean *(inset)*. After the first major battle of the war was fought across McLean's land near Manassas Junction, he moved his family to the quiet community of Appomattox Court House to avoid further contact with the war. By coincidence, when Lee asked staff member Colonel Charles Marshall to find a suitable meeting place for himself and Grant, Marshall prevailed upon McLean, and the historic event took place in McLean's parlor on April 8, 1865.

On April 12, 1865, Major General John B. Gordon *(left)*, led the remnant of the Confederate Army of Northern Virginia to lay down its arms at Appomattox Court House. Receiving the surrender was Brigadier General Joshua Lawrence Chamberlain, *(right)* who ordered his men to salute their gallant foe; Gordon returned the honor. Both commanders were volunteers who had served from the start of the war, and both had recovered from severe wounds to return to the fighting. Gordon went on to become governor of Georgia and a U.S. senator. Chamberlain served as governor of Maine and president of Bowdoin College.

"{Chamberlain} called his men into line and as my men marched in front of them, the veterans in blue gave a soldierly salute to those vanquished heros–a token of respect from Americans to Americans."
Major General John B. Gordon

"At the sound of that machine-like snap of arms, General Gordon started...{then} wheeled his horse, facing me, touching him gently with the spur so that the animal slightly reared, and, as he wheeled, horse and rider made one motion, the horse's head swung down with a graceful bow, and General Gordon dropped his sword-point to his toe in salutation."
Brigadier General Joshua Lawrence Chamberlain

December

SUNDAY

14

MONDAY - *1864 Battle of Nashville, Tennessee, begins*

15

TUESDAY - *1864 Battle of Nashville, Tennessee, ends*

16

WEDNESDAY

17

THURSDAY

18

FRIDAY

19

SATURDAY - *1860 South Carolina secedes*
1862 Confederate raid on Holly Springs, Mississippi

20

December

SUNDAY
21

MONDAY
22

TUESDAY
23

WEDNESDAY - HANUKKAH
24

THURSDAY - CHRISTMAS
25

FRIDAY - *1860 Federal garrison transfers to Fort Sumter*
26

SATURDAY
27

Snow blankets cavalry stables at Giesboro Point, south of Washington, D.C.

"This is Christmas evening but there is very little appearance of any frolicks...this has been spent as a kind of holy day...W. Frasier, W. J. Hill & I went to try and buy some turkey or chicken but failed in that so we just come back and tried it the old way on crackers & pork with a few beans & etc."
Letter from Corporal James Garvin Crawford, 80th Illinois
Infantry, to his parents, December 25, 1862

A member of the 8th Regiment Pennsylvania Volunteer Corps holds a beloved battle flag.

December

SUNDAY
28

MONDAY - *1862 BATTLE OF CHICKASAW BAYOU, MISSISSIPPI*
29

TUESDAY
30

WEDNESDAY - *1862 BATTLE OF STONES RIVER (MURFREESBORO), TENNESSEE*
WEST VIRGINIA ADMITTED TO THE UNION
31

"The war will be a great benefit, I think...if it end in nothing more than... making us appreciate peace and all it brings."
Lieutenant John H. Chamberlayne, 21st Virginia Infantry, August 16, 1861

"No more suffering, no more scenes of carnage and death. Thank God it is over and that the Union is restored. And so at last I am a simple citizen. Well, I am content, but should my country call again I am ready to respond."
Colonel Elisha H. Rhodes, 2d Rhode Island Volunteers, July 28, 1865

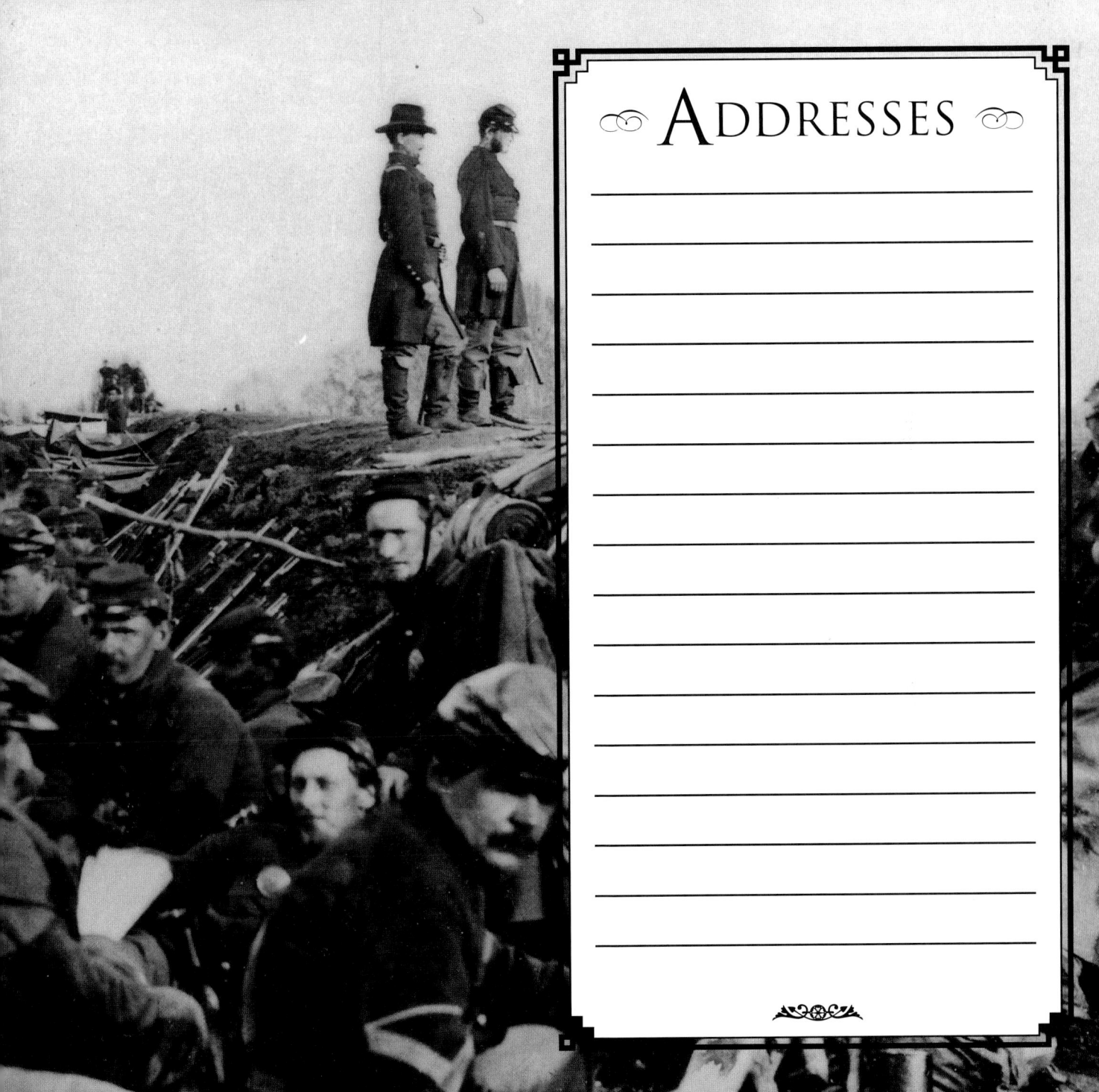

Addresses

ADDRESSES

ADDRESSES

Addresses

Addresses

Addresses

Addresses

Addresses

Addresses

BIRTHDAYS & ANNIVERSARIES

BIRTHDAYS & ANNIVERSARIES

BIRTHDAYS & ANNIVERSARIES

1997

JANUARY
S	M	T	W	T	F	S
			1	2	3	4
5	6	7	8	9	10	11
12	13	14	15	16	17	18
19	20	21	22	23	24	25
26	27	28	29	30	31	

FEBRUARY
S	M	T	W	T	F	S
						1
2	3	4	5	6	7	8
9	10	11	12	13	14	15
16	17	18	19	20	21	22
23	24	25	26	27	28	

MARCH
S	M	T	W	T	F	S
						1
2	3	4	5	6	7	8
9	10	11	12	13	14	15
16	17	18	19	20	21	22
23	24	25	26	27	28	29
30	31					

APRIL
S	M	T	W	T	F	S
		1	2	3	4	5
6	7	8	9	10	11	12
13	14	15	16	17	18	19
20	21	22	23	24	25	26
27	28	29	30			

MAY
S	M	T	W	T	F	S
				1	2	3
4	5	6	7	8	9	10
11	12	13	14	15	16	17
18	19	20	21	22	23	24
25	26	27	28	29	30	31

JUNE
S	M	T	W	T	F	S
1	2	3	4	5	6	7
8	9	10	11	12	13	14
15	16	17	18	19	20	21
22	23	24	25	26	27	28
29	30					

JULY
S	M	T	W	T	F	S
		1	2	3	4	5
6	7	8	9	10	11	12
13	14	15	16	17	18	19
20	21	22	23	24	25	26
27	28	29	30	31		

AUGUST
S	M	T	W	T	F	S
					1	2
3	4	5	6	7	8	9
10	11	12	13	14	15	16
17	18	19	20	21	22	23
24	25	26	27	28	29	30
31						

SEPTEMBER
S	M	T	W	T	F	S
	1	2	3	4	5	6
7	8	9	10	11	12	13
14	15	16	17	18	19	20
21	22	23	24	25	26	27
28	29	30				

OCTOBER
S	M	T	W	T	F	S
			1	2	3	4
5	6	7	8	9	10	11
12	13	14	15	16	17	18
19	20	21	22	23	24	25
26	27	28	29	30	31	

NOVEMBER
S	M	T	W	T	F	S
						1
2	3	4	5	6	7	8
9	10	11	12	13	14	15
16	17	18	19	20	21	22
23	24	25	26	27	28	29
30						

DECEMBER
S	M	T	W	T	F	S
	1	2	3	4	5	6
7	8	9	10	11	12	13
14	15	16	17	18	19	20
21	22	23	24	25	26	27
28	29	30	31			

1998

JANUARY
S	M	T	W	T	F	S
				1	2	3
4	5	6	7	8	9	10
11	12	13	14	15	16	17
18	19	20	21	22	23	24
25	26	27	28	29	30	31

FEBRUARY
S	M	T	W	T	F	S
1	2	3	4	5	6	7
8	9	10	11	12	13	14
15	16	17	18	19	20	21
22	23	24	25	26	27	28

MARCH
S	M	T	W	T	F	S
1	2	3	4	5	6	7
8	9	10	11	12	13	14
15	16	17	18	19	20	21
22	23	24	25	26	27	28
29	30	31				

APRIL
S	M	T	W	T	F	S
			1	2	3	4
5	6	7	8	9	10	11
12	13	14	15	16	17	18
19	20	21	22	23	24	25
26	27	28	29	30		

MAY
S	M	T	W	T	F	S
					1	2
3	4	5	6	7	8	9
10	11	12	13	14	15	16
17	18	19	20	21	22	23
24	25	26	27	28	29	30
31						

JUNE
S	M	T	W	T	F	S
	1	2	3	4	5	6
7	8	9	10	11	12	13
14	15	16	17	18	19	20
21	22	23	24	25	26	27
28	29	30				

JULY
S	M	T	W	T	F	S
			1	2	3	4
5	6	7	8	9	10	11
12	13	14	15	16	17	18
19	20	21	22	23	24	25
26	27	28	29	30	31	

AUGUST
S	M	T	W	T	F	S
						1
2	3	4	5	6	7	8
9	10	11	12	13	14	15
16	17	18	19	20	21	22
23	24	25	26	27	28	29
30	31					

SEPTEMBER
S	M	T	W	T	F	S
		1	2	3	4	5
6	7	8	9	10	11	12
13	14	15	16	17	18	19
20	21	22	23	24	25	26
27	28	29	30			

OCTOBER
S	M	T	W	T	F	S
				1	2	3
4	5	6	7	8	9	10
11	12	13	14	15	16	17
18	19	20	21	22	23	24
25	26	27	28	29	30	31

NOVEMBER
S	M	T	W	T	F	S
1	2	3	4	5	6	7
8	9	10	11	12	13	14
15	16	17	18	19	20	21
22	23	24	25	26	27	28
29	30					

DECEMBER
S	M	T	W	T	F	S
		1	2	3	4	5
6	7	8	9	10	11	12
13	14	15	16	17	18	19
20	21	22	23	24	25	26
27	28	29	30	31		

PICTURE CREDITS

BIBLIOGRAPHY

BOOKS

Alleman, Tillie (Pierce). *At Gettysburg, or What a Girl Saw and Heard of the Battle*. New York: W. Lake Borland, 1889.

Aptheker, Herbert, ed. *A Documentary History of the Negro People in the United States*. Vol. 1. New York: Citadel Press, 1979.

Conklin, E. F. *Women at Gettysburg, 1863*. Gettysburg, Pa.: Thomas Publications, 1993.

Davis, William C., and Bell I. Wiley, eds. *Photographic History of the Civil War*. New York: Black Dog and Leventhal, 1994.

Donald, David,ed., *Divided We Fought: A Pictorial History of the War, 1861-1865*.
New York: Macmillan, 1952.

Fellman, Michael. *Citizen Sherman: A Life of William Tecumseh Sherman*.
New York: Random House, 1995.

Gardner, Alexander. *Gardner's Photographic Sketch Book*. New York: Dover, 1959.

Key, William. *The Battle of Atlanta and the Georgia Campaign*. Atlanta: Peachtree, 1981.

Kunhardt, Phillip B., Jr., Philip B. Kunhardt III, and Peter W. Kunhardt. *Lincoln: An Illustrated Biography*. New York: Alfred A. Knopf, 1992.

Phillips, Charles, and Alan Axelrod. *My Brother's Face: Portraits of the Civil War in Photographs, Diaries and Letters*. San Francisco: Chronicle Books, 1993.

Rhodes, Robert Hunt, ed. *All for the Union: The Civil War Diary and Letters of Elisha Hunt Rhodes*. New York: Orion Books, 1991.

Sullivan, Constance, ed. *Landscapes of the Civil War*. New York: Alfred A. Knopf, 1995.

Ward, Geoffrey C. *The Civil War: An Illustrated History*. New York: Alfred A Knopf, 1990.